KIDISMS

Other books by Cathy Hamilton

Momisms
Dadisms

KIDISMS

WHAT THEY SAY AND WHAT THEY REALLY MEAN

Cathy Hamilton

**Andrews McMeel
Publishing**

Kansas City

03 04 05 06 07 BID 10 9 8 7 6 5 4 3 2 1

Library of Congress Cataloging-in-Publication Data

Hamilton, Cathy.
  Kidisms : what they say and what they really mean / Cathy Hamilton.
     p. cm.
  ISBN 0-7407-3956-5
  1. Child psychology. 2. Interpersonal communication in children.
3. Parent and child—Humor. 4. Parent and teenager—Humor.
5. Communication in the family. I. Title.

HQ772.H82 2003
305.231—dc22

                                                         2003057731

Book design by Holly Camerlinck
Composition by Steve Brooker

Attention: Schools and Businesses

Andrews McMeel books are available at quantity discounts with bulk purchase for educational, business, or sales promotional use. For information, please write to: Special Sales Department, Andrews McMeel Publishing, 4520 Main Street, Kansas City, Missouri 64111.

To my kids, Barrett and Emily,
with thanks for the endless material.

It's ridiculous how much I love you.

Introduction

Beginning with a baby's first delivery room cry, parents wait with bated breath for the first word. For the first twelve months or so of an infant's life, parents hang on desperately to every babble and burble, trying to interpret their child's premature verbal emissions as anything remotely intelligible. ("Honey, did you hear that? He just said 'Republican party!'")

Yes, the first word is an exciting milestone, indeed. Important enough to be documented in baby books, captured on videotape, and relayed in e-mails, letters, and Christmas cards to relatives and distant relations.

Soon, the more ambitious adults rush out and invest hundreds of dollars in picture books in an effort to teach the child every word under the sun in ninety days or less—"What is this?" "What does a cow say?" "How does a bird go?" "Can you say *cabernet savignon*?" These relentless vocabulary lessons can make even the most even-tempered baby suffer a major breakdown and shout out his first paragraph at the top of his lungs: "Enough already! Harvard or no Harvard, I'm having a meltdown here!"

But parents eventually learn that the first word leads to the second, and then the third, and soon, the child has a vocabulary of hundreds of words that he never stops using! Then, and only then, do parents wonder why they were ever in such a hurry to hear their babies speak in the first place.

Kids do say the darnedest things. Just ask Art Linkletter and Bill Cosby.

And some of the most darnedest things they say over and over and over—ad nauseam. Even as their young brains are developing vocabularies of hundreds, even thousands of words, you can expect the following expressions to pepper their conversations repeatedly throughout their formative years.

Some of these sayings are quite endearing.

Most, however, can just drive you nuts.

STAGE ONE:

BABYISMS

"Dada!"

Much to a mother's dismay, most babies learn to say *dada* before *mama*. Speech and language experts explain the phenomenon simply, reasoning that the *d* sound is easier to pronounce than the *m* sound. Still, moms tend to take this as a personal affront until they hear the baby calling anyone with trousers and facial hair by the title, including the mail carrier, butcher, and parish priest.

"Bye-bye!"

Adults love to hear a baby say *bye-bye* and will often refuse to end a visit until they've gotten the brief but intense satisfaction of multiple *bye-bye*s from a willing, or unwilling, infant. Instead, they'll stand and wait, with endless patience, cajoling the baby with funny little waves. "Say bye-bye! BYE-bye! C'mon, say it! Bye-bye!"

The discriminating baby will hold back, teasing, taunting, and reserving his *bye-bye*s for a select few adults (usually the ones who aren't making fools of themselves).

But the eager-to-please baby will *bye-bye* for anyone and everyone, garnering big smiles, and often applause, in return. Occasionally, these babies will fall into a repetitive pattern of *bye-bye*s that can be difficult to break, uttering *bye-bye* ten, twenty, even thirty times in one night. Many of these babies grow up to be flight attendants.

"More!"

Parents would be advised to get used to this kidism as this request will repeat itself approximately 1,266,548 times before the child becomes a legal adult. More cereal, more dessert, more presents, more clothes, more Legos, more earrings, more makeup, more shoes, more CDs, more bicycles, more cars, more money, more money, more money...

"No!"

The oft-repeated "No!" is the first sign of a baby sensing his own power. To refuse something and to shock one's parents at the same time is a major milestone and a heady experience in a young child's life, one too wonderfully addictive to do just once or twice. That's why during certain phases of life (the terrible twos and the terrible teens) this kidism will get a real workout.

"Now!"

Having tasted the deliciousness of a good hearty *no*, a baby will test the waters with more and more demands. You can expect to hear the above kidism emphatically punctuating such requests as "More ice cream!" and "Put me down!"

"I do it!"

Babies' lives are remarkably dependent, adults being responsible for their very survival and, in large part, their comfort and entertainment. This is fine, if the baby is lucky enough to have entertaining adults around. Unfortunately, some babies aren't so lucky. Is it any wonder, then, that young children are so adamant about doing something—anything—by themselves? If just for the sheer entertainment value of it?

"I am *not* a baby!"

Mature toddlers of, say, three or three and a half, become downright indignant when referred to as "baby." That's why adults should take care not to say things like "Put the baby down for a nap" or "Somebody watch the baby. . . . We're going to get a room."

"Mama!"

When a baby finally figures out how to purse her lips in just the right way to say *mama*, many mothers will literally weep with joy. But the tears dry quickly when "Mama" quickly becomes a 700-times-a-day clingy cry for attention.

"Huh?"

{ This is the sound your baby makes when you replace his binky with an educational toy. }

"Ga ga, goo goo."

Except in the case of cartoon babies (which aren't real, by the way), the phrase "Ga ga, goo goo" rarely escapes an infant's lips. But I suspect that if it did, the translation would be something like: "Why does everyone keep saying things twice to me?"

"I gotta boo-boo."

Otherwise known as an *ouchie*, a *boo-boo* is a cut, scrape, or abrasion, and a baby's ticket to receive an inordinate amount of sympathy from adults. All a baby needs to do is open her eyes wide, jut out her bottom lip, and present her boo-boo to a receptive adult, then sit back and reap the rewards:

"Oh, poor baby. That's a terrible boo-boo. Baby want some ice cream? Cookies? How about a five-dollar bill?"

Some babies have been known to milk their boo-boos long enough to earn a full year's college tuition.

14

"Waaaaaaaaaaaaaaaaaaaaaaa!"

Usually reserved for those inopportune moments in the harsh glare of the public eye, like a grocery-store line, a baby can wail a "Waaaaaaaaaaaaaaaaaaa" for an astonishing length of time without breathing.

Make no mistake. When this happens, your baby is *not* a happy camper. And the bluer his face becomes, the more certain you can be about this.

15

Most experts recommend parents ignore a baby in the throes of a full-blown tantrum. But veterans of such checkout line dramas recommend Reese's Peanut Butter Cups ten-to-one as a sure cure.

"Peekaboo."

If there's one way to get instant gratification from an adult, any adult, it's to play peekaboo. Babies learn from an early age that this little cause-and-effect exercise can be incredibly rewarding, garnering cookies, kisses, and big laughs from seemingly simpleminded grandparents.

16

"Me first!"

Most children, no matter how agreeable in other areas of their life, hate—and I mean *hate*—to go second, third, or, heaven forbid, last! At the drinking fountain, on the swing, at the electric rocking horse outside of Wal-Mart, a child's first priority is to be the lead dog of the pack.

The one exception to this rule is in the doctor's office at booster shot time. Then a child will become amazingly magnanimous, offering: "No, that's okay. After you!"

17

"My turn!"

> If a child is denied the privilege of going first, it will only be a matter of a few seconds before this kidism is voiced in no uncertain terms. Kids are adamant about getting equal time—equal time in this case meaning more time than the kids before and after him.

"All gone!"

Here's another cause-and-effect game that babies find very amusing. Baby drinks all of her milk and says, "All gone!" Adults go crazy. Baby eats all of her cereal and says, "All gone!" Adults go crazy. Baby pours a full cup of milk on the floor and says, "All gone." Adults say, "Game over."

"That's more better."

Don't dismay if your child doesn't practice perfect grammar right away. The English language is one of the most complicated on earth to learn, with hundreds of rules and just as many exceptions to those rules.

20

However, if your child is still using
this phrase past the fourth grade,
you've got a problem.

"Watch me!"

Some kids are born exhibitionists and will insist on having an audience every time they jump off the side of the pool, perform a somersault, even go to the bathroom. Parents are happy to comply with their wishes and will watch, cheer, and even applaud—until about the hundredth time.

STAGE TWO:

kIDisms

"He started it!"

The number-one objective of all children is to avoid blame at all costs. That's why you'll never walk in on a bedroom brawl to hear your son say, "No, no! It's *my* fault! Geez, when will I ever learn to stop picking fights? Mom, please! Take away my privileges quick so that I might break this vicious cycle!"

"I can do it by myself."

{ We all want children who adamantly strive for independence, don't we? And so, when a child insists he can do something by himself—tie his shoes, zip his coat, put on his pajamas—we wait patiently for him to accomplish his task no matter how long it takes. }

26

Until we lose our minds and
have to help the klutzy kid out.

"Where do babies come from?"

Here's a kidism that strikes fear into the hearts of parents everywhere. Psychologists recommend answering the dreaded query with honesty and plain anatomical language, providing as much information as the child seems to need and avoiding such traditional but mythical explanations as storks, pumpkin seeds, and UPS trucks.

For some reason, over 50 percent of parents still ignore this advice.

"But Dad already said I could!"

A kid is in finest form when she's playing one parent against the other, and the above ism is a common tactic used to divide and conquer.

This classic form of manipulation is easily mastered by any five-year-old with average intelligence. Here's the drill:

Child to Dad: *Can* I spend the night with Tiffany?

Dad to Child: If it's **okay** with your mother, it's **okay** with me.

Child to Mom: *Can* I spend the night with Tiffany?

Mom to Child: No. You have softball practice in the morning.

Child to Mom: But *Dad* already said I could!

29

By playing both sides of the house, as it were,
a kid can improve her chances of getting
a "yes" by 50 percent. Why? Because she
knows Mom will never veto Dad—at least
on the small stuff.

"I know you are, but what am I?"

This little ditty is a kid's standard retort to name-calling like "Stupid," "Weenie," and the ever-popular "Butthead." It's relatively harmless as an outdoor exercise, but parents should never allow this ism to be uttered inside a moving vehicle, as the volley could go on forever:

30

"Big *fat* baby!"

"I know you are, but what am I?"

"Poopy head pigface."

"I know you are, but what am I?"

"Sniffling *wussy* nose!"

"I know you are, but what am I?"

"I know *you* are, but what am I?"

"I know *you* are, but what am I?"

"You are!"

"No, *you* are!" . . .

"I forgot."

32

It's ten thirty on Sunday night and your son has just announced that he has a major science project due in the morning that's worth 70 percent of his grade. Your face turns blue as you ask how this could possibly happen, again! And he answers you, with that pathetic look on his face, "I forgot."

Under these circumstances, 10 percent of parents will spew out some words of wisdom: "You made your bed, now lie in it" and go back to bed. The remaining schmucks will trod off to the kitchen to find the glue and toothpicks.

"Are we there yet?"

It's a well-known fact that children under the age of twenty have no concept of time or distance, especially while traveling cross-country without the calming effects of an Enya CD or Auto Bingo. The average kid will ask this question or its equally annoying counterpart— "How many more minutes?"—every five to ten miles, unless his parents explain the estimated time of arrival in terms he can comprehend:

"Okay, pay attention. We left our house at the beginning of *Sesame Street* and we need to drive through *Blue's Clues, Barney, I Love Lucy,* and *The Gong Show.* We won't arrive at the hotel until the end of Nick at Nite. Got it?"

"It wasn't me!"

There has been a crash. The window suddenly has a gaping hole in it. Your daughter is standing on the lawn surrounded by shards of broken glass, baseball bat still in hand. There is not another kid in sight for seventeen miles. If you are dumb enough to ask, "Who broke the window?" you deserve to hear the above ism.

34

"P.U. What stinks?"

Kids' noses are almost as sensitive as their mothers'. They can pick up offensive odors from miles away, especially bodily emissions. Unlike their mothers, however, kids feel an inexplicable urge to comment in excruciatingly graphic detail about every remotely strange smell:

35

"**Phew!** What smells like rotten eggs?"

"Somebody **forgot to wipe!**"

"Who *puked* in the chili?"

"**Ew!** This casserole smells like catfood!"

"I'm·bored.
There's nothing to do."

Even with a five-thousand-dollar play struc-
ture in the backyard, big-screen TV, dozens of
video games, 2,783,988 Legos in the closet,
scooters, bikes, and ten kids living within two
hundred feet of their front door, kids will utter
this gem on the average of 3.4 times per day.
Sixteen times per day in the summertime.

36

"Nothing."

{ This is what you're likely to hear when your child is behind a locked bathroom door with the cat, your best pair of scissors, and a blow dryer, and you ask, "What's going on in there?" }

"I already did my homework."
"I don't have any homework."

{ Psychological studies have shown that kids will lie for two reasons: }

38

1. To **avoid** punishment.

2. To **avoid** homework, the most *horrendous* form of punishment of all.

"You're the worst mom/dad in the world."

{ Don't be hurt or offended when your child throws this one at you. Remember, it's all relative, especially when you consider the entire country thinks the Osbournes are Parents of the Year. }

"I'm running away from home and I'm never coming back!"

When a child makes this announcement, even as she's standing at the door, luggage in hand, a parent's first inclination is to use reverse psychology and say something like "Don't forget to write" or "Don't let the door hit you in the butt on the way out."

Sometimes, though, this strategy backfires, and a parent will find herself racing to the bus station, trying to stop the 5:15 to Los Angeles.

"We weren't doing anything bad!"

{ You know you've walked in on a crime in progress when a kid blurts out this kidism the second you open his bedroom door! }

41

"My stomach hurts."

This classic kidism can mean one of two things:

1. The child's stomach does, in fact, hurt, indicating a gastrointestinal problem of major or minor proportions.

2. An age-old tactic designed to avoid unpleasantries such as school, chores, trips to Grandma's, or orthodontist appointments.

The best tack to take in both scenarios is to fetch an empty bowl, suspend consumption of all solid food, and put said child in bed with instructions not to eat anything for twenty-four hours. If the kid's faking it, she'll last approximately two hours past the first missed meal.

42

"Why do I have to make my bed? I'm just going to sleep in it later."

{ Kids are amazingly adept at pointing out how ridiculous some of our adult rituals and conventions really are. Logic like this makes parenting difficult, if not impossible. }

43

Unfortunately,
this ism does make a point.

"I'm thirsty!
I need a drink of water!"

44

There is a strange but all-too-common phenomenon that occurs when children are put to bed for the night. An extreme and unquenchable thirst comes over them like nightfall on the Sahara desert. Suddenly, their little mouths turn to cotton, their tongues swell, lips pucker, and nothing, but nothing, will remedy their parched tongues but a tall glass of water, and they are forced to cry out in the night: "I'm thirsty!"

This commonly occurs precisely twelve minutes after the final good-night kiss, when the parent has climbed down the stairs, poured himself a nightcap, and settled in to watch his favorite TV show.

Timing is everything with kids.

"But Susie's mom is letting her!"

Savvy kids know there is usually one permissive parent respected enough by her fellow parents to be the trendsetter. And this ism is one way to employ parental peer pressure. Naming names, like Susie's mom, works only if she is a sage with Oprah-like wisdom and her child's best interest always at heart. However, if Susie's mom is the harlot of the Harper Valley PTA, this ism doesn't stand a chance.

45

"We promise not to fight."

The most effective way to force affection between two squabbling siblings or friends is to tell them they can't play together anymore. Do this and you'll see a pair of seething and snarling playmates turn lovey-dovey in a matter of seconds as they take the above ism pledge, often with arms wrapped around each others' shoulders.

Don't believe this for a minute.

In fact, it's a good idea never to expect a kid to keep any promise. Ever.

"I'll never ever do it again."
Or "I've learned my lesson."

Muttered through streams of tears and chok-
ing sobs, this ism is a kid's desperate attempt
to avoid punishment or at least achieve a
lesser sentence. Again, don't be fooled. Kids'
promises are as fleeting as a politician's. They'll
say anything to save their TV privileges.

47

"I'll be your best friend!"

A child wants something. A turn on the tire swing. An invitation to a birthday party. A classmate's half-eaten sandwich at the lunch table. The child has no money and few material possessions of his own to barter, so he offers the next best thing—the coveted privilege of being his "best friend"—as a bargaining chip.

48

"He pushed me first!"

The best offense is a good defense. Kids understand this instinctively. This ism is a child's first usage of the self-defense defense. Many who use this tack successfully go on to become brilliant lawyers.

"Is this my right or my left?"

Early childhood specialists advise there is nothing to worry about if a child occasionally confuses his right and his left. The brain's right and left hemispheres take a few years to establish their function in the average child and a little confusion is perfectly normal.

But if your child is still posing the above question days before his driving test, better get him a bus pass.

50

"But I'm not hungry!!"

Kids' appetites are fickle creatures. The harder parents push ("Eat your vegetables." "Clean your plate." "There are starving children in Third World countries!"), the less hungry a kid seems to get. Of course, get a kid within five miles of a Dairy Queen or the golden arches and you'll hear the following ism . . .

51

"I'm staaaarving!!"

When the door slams at three thirty in the afternoon on a school day, before you hear the backpack hit the floor and the shoes flinging across the room and the TV warming up, you're certain to hear the above ism. And, often, so will the neighbors.

52

"How do you spell _____?"

Most kids will do anything to shorten the time it takes to finish their homework, including soliciting help from their exasperated parents. When this ism ends with a word like *prestidigitation*, parents should insist the child look the word up in the dictionary.

But when a child asks "How do you spell *the?*" it could be time for a remedial spelling lesson.

53

"But I can't look it up if I don't know how to spell it!"

This "gotcha" response to a parent's urging to "look it up in the dictionary" is impossible to argue with. Don't even try.

54

"I can't wear *this*. It itches!"

Your kid can withstand fifty oozing mosquito bites, roll around in the sticker bushes without batting an eye, and skip happily through the poison ivy. But the minute he puts on a new sweater or church clothes he suddenly becomes Mr. Sensitive, fidgeting and scratching like he's being attacked by an army of red ants.

This itchy-clothing syndrome is a phenomenon caused by expensive new sweaters, suits, ties, and shirts with collars.

"I didn't hit him, he hit me!"

The "him" in question could be beaten to a bloody pulp, lying in a crumpled heap in the corner, requiring reconstructive rhinoplasty, while your kid doesn't have a scratch on him. Still, he will try to convince you that it was a matter of self-defense.

Note to parents:

Starting saving for law school.

"She won't share!"

Just like burglars, kids can't resist the temptation of another's property, especially if it's a
new toy. When the other child won't give it
up, you're bound to hear this one in various
degrees of whine.

"Why can't I? It's a free country."

You gotta love the democracy argument, especially when it comes from an underage, dependent, unemployed child whose very survival and livelihood depends entirely on his overage, overtaxed parents.

58

"Girls (boys) are gross!"

Every young child goes through a period of loathing the opposite sex. Unfortunately, most of them outgrow this phase, leading to a whole slew of new problems. Therefore, it is recommended that parents support, if not encourage, the idea of girls (or boys) being gross for as long as possible.

"Ew. She's got cooties!"

Webster's definition:

Cootie *(n)*: a louse feeding primarily on the body; *especially* : a sucking louse (*Pediculus humanus*) feeding on the body and living in the clothing of humans.

Your eight-year-old son's definition:

Cootie *(n)*: What that gross Amanda Nilty's got.

More likely to be found in elementary school–age girls, cooties are considered contagious and often require self "vaccinations" like intense arm punching or pinching.

"It was an accident!"

{
What kid in his right mind is going to admit he broke a vase, window, or his brother's nose on purpose?
}

"But whyyyyyyyy?"

When a child resorts to this sing-songy drone, his goal isn't really to find out the reason for something. It's to annoy the parent so completely and thoroughly that he or she gives in to the child's unreasonable request.

"But whyyyyy?" may be the most irritating question on earth, especially when asked by an unrelentingly whining child in the line at Costco. The tot-mother exchange goes something like this:

Child: Mom, can I have some candy?

Mom: No.

Child: *But why?*

Mom: Because it's bad for your teeth.

Child (getting louder): *But whyyyy?*

Mom: Because sugar causes tooth decay.

Child *(agitated now): But whyyyyyy?*

Mom: Because sugar turns into plaque, which eats into the enamel.

Child *(in full whine mode): But whyyyyyyyy?*

Mom: Because plaque, when left unchecked, creates bacteria, which contain acid that eats into the tooth's hard surface . . .

Child *(breaking the sound barrier): But whyyyyyyyyyy?*

63

It is strongly recommended at this point, before others in the express lane jump-vault over the conveyor belt and take matters into their own hands, that the mother say, with all the authority she can command, "Because I said so, *that's whyyyyyyyyyyyyy!*"

"I'm not scared."

This defiant declaration is used to convince skeptical parents that a kid is ready to perform such daring feats as viewing a horror movie or spending the night alone in the backyard in a brand-new pup tent.

"I'm scared."

{ This is what the same kid will murmur in a whisper as he climbs into your bed at 10:30 the same night. }

"You love her more than me!"

No matter how hard you try to convince your children that you love them equally, some kids are always looking for signs of partisanship. Those signs include bigger helpings of mashed potatoes, later bedtimes, and more Christmas presents.

66

This is just one of the reasons
why parents can never win.

"That's not what you said last week!"

Leave it to a kid who can't remember her own lunch to be able to regurgitate verbatim what a parent said in a weak moment one week ago. This tack is 99 percent effective since the typical mom will be unable to remember what she said this morning, let alone a whole week ago.

67

"No fair!"

{ The list of things considered unfair by kids is never-ending. Here, at last count, is the Top 20: }

1. homework

2. chores

3. taking turns

4. curfews

5. Sunday school

6. braces

7. early bedtime on school nights

8. sharing

9. strict baby-sitters

10. saving half of one's allowance

11. sharing a bedroom with a sibling

12. doing dishes

13. picking up the bathroom

14. cleaning one's room before going out to play

15. under-the-bed inspections

16. pop quizzes

17. limiting dessert to one piece per person

18. punishments of all kinds

19. parental-control devices on the TV

20. healthy snacks

69

"You're embarrassing me!"

{ A parent is sure to hear this ism when engaging in the following behavior: }

70

singing aloud and head-banging to
"Wild Thing" while driving carpool

clapping loudly, yelling "Woo woo!"
in the middle of the school play

wearing an outfit that shows more
bare skin than her hands and feet

wearing **black socks** with his
sandals to the Little League game

kissing said child anywhere
on his or her person

hugging said child anywhere
but at home

making eye contact with said child anywhere
but in the privacy of his or her own room

"Can I come out now?"

Sending a child to his room will afford you on the average 6.3 minutes of precious silence. Then, don't be surprised to hear this ism in the sweetest, most syrupy voice you've ever heard.

"I'm on strike!"

It's hard not to admire the kid who tries this one to avoid work. Some of the more theatrical kids will go the full route: making protest signs, marching on a picket line in the driveway, chanting "Hell no! I won't mow!"

Most of these young strikers, however, make a hasty retreat into the house when management holds firm and his siblings turn into scabs.

73

"Shut up!"

No mother worth her salt would allow her child to say "Shut up!" (Mom reserves that privilege for herself, to use on Dad.)

"Jason's got a girlfriend! Jason's got a girlfriend!"

The fastest way to create a sensation, if not a total scandal, in a family is to announce to one and all that your older sibling is involved in a romantic relationship. Experienced younger siblings will break this kind of news only at the dinner table, when their parents are on hand to protect them from the inevitable pummeling.

75

"Pleeeeease!"

The record for the most *pleases* uttered by one child in a single day is 1,277. This was set by a five-year-old girl in Spokane, Washington, whose repeated pleas for her two hundred and fourteenth Beanie Baby caused a severe case of laryngitis, requiring hospital care.

"Will you leave the light on?"

Kids have a love-hate relationship with the dark. The dark is great for forts and scary movies when you're in the company of your peers. The dark is not so great when you're all alone with only your memories of Freddy Krueger to keep you company.

"There's a monster in my closet."

You know there's no monster in his closet. Psychologists know there's no monster in his closet. Even *he* knows, at some level, there is no monster in his closet. But when you hear this ism at three in the morning, and reason and logic have left the building to find Elvis, cast child psychology to the wind and let the kid hop into bed with you.

78

"I hate you."

When these three horrendous words escape their precious baby's lips for the first time, parents receive it like a knife to the gut. This unsavory kidism is yet another attempt at shock value, and it usually hits the mark.

What the kid wants to say isn't really "I hate you." It's more like "I am really, really angry, and since you taught me not to swear, this is the worst thing I can possibly think of. So there!"

"But I'm allergic to peas*!"

When face-to-face with a vegetable or fruit that is unfamiliar, unattractive, or just plain gross, a child can develop anticipatory psychosomatic nonallergic gastrointestinal rhinitis. That is, a condition that causes a severe reaction prior to the actual ingestion of said food. This is why a child can actually break out in hives, gasping "Call the ambulance" with shortened breath, before the offending food ever touches his lips.

80

*Substitute with:

**broccoli • lima beans • cauliflower
okra • Brussels sprouts • beets
cabbage • spinach • bok choy
cantaloupe • honeydew melon • prunes**

"I *am* telling the truth!"

Pinocchio notwithstanding, most kids are sure they have the ability and confidence to tell a baldface lie and get away with it, even when their eyes are shifting, their knees are quaking, and their faces are turning beet red.

"If you let me do it just this one time, I promise I'll never ask again."

When a kid has been harping relentlessly to do something you don't want him to do, he'll likely resort to this ism, knowing the payoff of having him actually shut up might persuade you to cave, just this once. Don't fall for it! Remember, it's a promise, and kid promises are as good as mold.

82

"She keeps coming over to my side of the room!"

Kids are territorial creatures, especially if they have a sibling, close in age, with whom they have to share a room, a bed, or the backseat of a car. In their desperate attempt to have their own space they'll often resort to literally dividing a room, sofa, or car seat into exactly equal halves.

Some kids use an imaginary line, while others have been known to use yellow crime-scene tape, spray paint, or orange highway cones. If a child goes to trouble of this extent, you can fully expect her to rant and rave when a sibling "crosses the line."

"I can't eat this! It's touching the other food!"

There are two kinds of young eaters: discriminatory and nondiscriminatory.

Nondiscriminatory eaters welcome any and all food groups and treat them equally, whether they commingle on the plate or not. These are the kids who instinctively mix strained peas with their pureed chicken with their mashed apples…and like it! These are your future chefs.

Discriminatory eaters are another matter. These kids are culinary segregationists who are likely to throw a holy fit if a milligram of mashed potato rubs up against one green bean. And casseroles? Fugeddaboutit! These are your future runway models and those likely to utter the above ism.

"You're the best mom in the whole wide world!"

{ Beware the child who starts a conversation with the above phrase, especially if he is hugging and kissing you while he's saying it. }

85

He wants something.
And it's going to be big.

"Who farted?"

For generations, kids have found flatulence to be the most fascinating of all bodily functions—disgusting and incredibly funny at the same time. It's a killer combination, especially to a kid.

The accusatory tone of this question implies that someone has passed gas and tried to get away with it. In the world of kids, if you're going to fart, you want to make a huge deal of it. Try a countdown, "pull my finger," something of that sort. Because if you try a "Silent but Deadly," you're liable to get busted, and then you'll never live it down.

"There's never anything to eat in this house."

You can have cupboards overflowing with cans, jars, and boxes of every staple imaginable. You can have a refrigerator jam-packed with seasonal produce, fresh-squeezed juice, dairy products, and condiments of all kinds. But unless you have a ready and endless supply of Chee-tos, Lucky Charms, Chips Ahoy, Skittles, Ho Hos, and Pringles on hand, you are bound to be assaulted with the above ism.

87

"Everybody else's mom is letting them."

Wouldn't it be fun to throw a weekly Everybody Else's Mom Convention? Then you could find out, once and for all, what kind of nonsense everybody else's kids are feeding these poor women.

"But everybody's doing it!"

If your child were to be believed, every kid in the sixth grade would be piercing her nipples, going steady, attending coed sleepovers, getting tattoos on her inner thighs, dying her hair the colors of Neopolitan ice cream, spending her spring break in Daytona Beach, seeing R-rated movies, and wearing thousands of dollars in cosmetics and fishnet stockings.

Where are we, anyway—"Girls Gone Wild" training camp?

"Right after this show..."

> Here's another example of children measuring time in TV show increments. When your little procrastinator gives you this put-off, just make sure he's not watching a two-week miniseries before you relent.

"Just ten more minutes!"

There isn't a little boy or girl on the planet who welcomes the words "Time for bed!" Parents who announce bedtime can expect a barrage of begging, pleading, and bargaining, even as the child's eyes are closing in spite of himself.

"But you guys get to stay up late!"

Oh, the unfairness of it all. Kids have to turn in to their warm, fluffy beds while grown-ups get to stay up doing laundry, paying bills, and making lunches for the next day.

Hey, that **is** unfair!

"Na na na boo boo!"

Sometimes followed by "You can't catch me," this classic taunt has been around for generations. No one knows exactly what it means, but linguists suspect its origins are with Yogi Bear and his sidekick, Boo Boo.

"You're not the boss of me."

{ The average child has at least six bosses, including mom, dad, teachers, principal, baby-sitters, and older siblings. }

94

So is it any wonder a kid rises up in
rebellion once in a while?

"I have to go to the bathroom."

Young bladders tend to act up at the most inopportune times—twenty minutes into a wedding ceremony, on an elevator, in line at the amusement park, at a five-star restaurant, five minutes after leaving a rest stop on the highway. With a fair amount of distraction, an older child's needs can be postponed until more opportune moments. Unless you hear . . .

"I have to go to the bathroom *now!*"

When a child says she has to go to the bathroom *now*, that means you have approximately five seconds to get her to the nearest restroom. The countdown begins with the word *now*.

"I can't sleep."

{ Unless the child has consumed mass quanti-
ties of Twinkies, Mountain Dew, sugar, or
caffeine since dinnertime, this ism can be
interpreted to mean: "I don't want to miss
Letterman." }

97

"But I'm not tired!"

There is nothing more stubborn (or pathetic) than a child who insists he's not tired enough for a nap, even after two consecutive days of soccer tournaments or a six A.M. swimming lesson, when he's yawning repeatedly and his eyes are closing no matter how hard he tries to hold them open.

"I can't eat it. I'll throw up!"

Once a child plants the notion of throwing up in her own head, you can be sure she can make it happen. Best not to force down that bite of spinach or polenta or you might have a little more dining-room drama on your hands than you wanted.

"Okay, but just *one* bite!"

This is a child giving in to your insistence that he or she take just one bite of a newly introduced food. Pay attention: Kids become magicians in making that one bite disappear—spitting it back out in a napkin, feeding it to the family dog under the table, or actually holding the bite inside their mouths until the end of the meal, when they sneakily deposit it in the trash.

"Can I sleep with you tonight?"

Woe to the parents who hear this ism from the darkened doorway of their master suite. Uttered with enough sympathy-provoking vulnerability, few parents can resist saying "Oh, all right, but just for tonight."

Be careful! This is a dangerous can of worms you're opening.

"I had a bad dream."

It's midnight. You and your spouse have just retired to the marital bed for a rare intimate encounter. Just as things start getting into gear, a little voice from the doorway utters this dreaded ism.

102

Oh, well. There's always next month.

"You don't love me anymore."

Kids do melodrama better than most actors on daytime TV. When yours tries this guilt-inducement on you, ask the question "What makes you say that?" You'll probably discover your alleged lack of love has something to do with your insistence on a ten o'clock curfew.

103

"I think I'm coming down with something."

{ **Translation:** An algebra test, overdue term paper, or church trip to a nursing home is coming down on *me*. }

"I think I have a fever."

In the classic fake-illness ploy, the savvy child knows a temperature above 98.6 is the holy grail—the point at which no school or day care center wants anything to do with them. Thanks to movies like *E.T.* and *Ferris Bueller's Day Off,* simulating a temperature has become an amateur art form. So before you fall for the old 101.4 on the oral thermometer, be sure to check for hot light bulbs, heating pads, or cups of hot tea in the vicinity of the child.

"My room *is* clean!"

Your definition of clean: toys and clothes picked up and put away, old food removed and taken to kitchen, bed made, furniture dusted, carpet vacuumed.

Your kid's definition of clean: moldy food shoved under the bed, path cleared from bed to door, closet doors shoved closed.

STAGE THREE:

TEENisms

"I *will!*"

You've asked your teen to pick up his room five times a day for the past week. Every time you ask him he answers, "I will." Finally, in frustration, you climb the stairs, knock on his door, step into his room, and ask in your sweetest, most nonthreatening tone, "Honey, aren't you ever going to clean this room?"

Suddenly, he turns and shouts, red-faced, "I *will!*" as if to say "How many times do I have to tell you?"

109

"It's not my fault."

It's never a teen's fault. It's the teacher's fault, a sibling's fault, the neighbor's fault, the school system's fault, the police's fault, the convenience-store clerk who sold him the cigarettes' fault, the friend's parents who left town for the weekend's fault.... You get the picture.

"Just drop me off at the corner."

When you hear this one, you know you've reached that precious stage in adolescence when your child no longer wants to be seen with you.

There is nothing more humiliating to an adolescent than getting dropped off at the mall or an event by his parents. That's why, at any given concert venue or multiplex, you'll see carloads of kids pouring out of minivans and SUVs, just to schlep five blocks to the front door. The long walk allows plenty of time for extra makeup application, hair combing, and wardrobe adjustment.

Who says kids don't make good use of their time?

111

"In a minute!"

In the real world, one minute equals sixty seconds. But in Teen World, real time is a concept grasped only by geeks with pocket protectors. When a teen says "in a minute," you can reasonably expect to wait a minimum of twenty minutes, or until dinner turns ice cold.

"Sor-ry!"

This is a teen's version of a sincere apology. Accept it. This is as good as it's going to get for a while.

"I don't remember."

Selective amnesia. It's the next best thing to taking the fifth. Kids who practice it grow into excellent material witnesses for the defense.

"Duh."

{ **Translation:** Of course. Naturally. Indeed. Indubitably. No doubt. }

"What!?!"

You can tell your teen is in "one of those moods" when you call his name sweetly and his voice comes bellowing back *"What!?!"* as if to say, *"What do you want now, you impossibly demanding nag? I just logged onto Dragon Slayer!"*

"I'll be out in a second!"

When a teenager locks herself in the bathroom, time seems to stand still. That's because the rest of us always underestimate the time it takes to put each individual hair into place, one by one.

"Don't you trust me?"

Mothers aren't the only ones fond of playing the guilt card. Teens are masterful at it. Kids will use this ism to shame parents into letting them go somewhere or do something that is clearly fraught with temptation. This question asks parents to somehow forget the past—speeding tickets, broken curfews, bad report cards, and so on—and give the child the benefit of the doubt. One more time.

"None of my other friends have to do chores."

If your teen is to be believed, families all over the neighborhood are employing maids, gardeners, and robots to do the dishes, mow the lawn, and take out the trash. "Chores" are for farm people, like cow-milking and hay-baling, and no self-respecting suburban urchin performs menial household tasks without monetary compensation.

119

Of course, this is the same teen who told you he was at the library studying last night.

"I *did* study! The teacher just doesn't like me."

According to some teens (who naturally know more than we do), teachers keep a secret blacklist of undesirable students who will never do better than a C on their report cards, no matter how well they perform in class.

Nobody knows why these students make the list. But when parents ask teachers to confirm this theory at conference time, they are often surprised to find out that their innocent victims have logged eight unexplained absences and seventeen missing homework assignments.

120

"It had gas in it when I brought it back!"

A strange phenomenon occurs when a teenager returns his parent's car to the garage after a night on the town. Sometime between midnight and the break of day, small gas-guzzling gremlins creep into the garage and siphon all but a few drops of fuel from the tank of the car. Most parents don't notice this until they are stranded on the side of the freeway, their gas gauge pointing to E.

"I am so *fat!*"

When a teenage girl who easily fits into size-seven jeans complains she's fat, a mom's first inclination is to swat her upside the head with a *Vogue* magazine. But keep in mind, it's terribly difficult for teenage girls these days, what with all the emaciated role models on billboards and movie screens.

A mother's first response is often to say "You're not fat. You're just big-boned." This rarely, if ever, works.

The best solution is to remove all full-length mirrors from the home during the teen years.

"You treat me like a child."

Parents should make every attempt not to laugh hysterically when their offspring challenges them with this ism. Especially when that offspring has just been caught redhanded attempting to ignite his flatulence with a lit match.

123

"What do I know? I'm just a kid!"

This is one of my personal favorites. Kids spend their whole lives trying to convince their parents they are old enough, mature enough, responsible enough, and smart enough to tackle adult responsibilities and reap adult rewards. But let a kid do something stupid like set the basement on fire with a bottle rocket, and you'll hear the above disclaimer.

124

"No. Nobody called while you were out."

Here's another puzzling case of selective adolescent memory. Even the world's brightest minds can't figure out how a teenager can remember every word that was said, verbatim, in a locker-hall lovers' quarrel two weeks ago, and still not be able to recall taking one simple phone message from your mechanic.

"Why do I smell like smoke? Everyone around me was smoking."

The secondhand smoke defense is hard to dispute unless a parent is willing to pry open the child's mouth and look for telltale nicotine stains on the teeth.

126

"They're not my cigarettes! I'm just holding them for somebody else."

Yes, well, this one makes sense, doesn't it? Because that's what friends in high school do, don't they? They put themselves in danger of being busted by their own parents so their no-good, nicotine-addicted friends can get on with their lives scot free!

"Okay, maybe I *was* smoking. But I didn't inhale!"

{ We can thank former President Clinton for this one. }

128

"I'm the only one who never gets to do anything."

This is a bold and often successful attempt to gain sympathy from parents by convincing them they are the *only* ones who are strict (read: mean and cruel) enough to prevent said child from having the time of his life at a concert, party, or PG-13 movie. The child assumes that the parent will automatically take his word for it and not contact other parents to confirm that they are not, in fact, equally mean and cruel.

129

"I was just about to call."

It is fifty minutes past curfew and still no sign of your teenager. You've been frantically dialing his cell phone, which is, inconveniently or strategically, turned off. Finally, you've utilized the emergency calling tree, waking up over a dozen parents from their much-needed sleep, and you have determined the whereabouts of your child. You call the house in question and wait several minutes while the message gets passed from one screaming teen to the next until finally, your teen arrives at the phone, at which time you will hear the above lame excuse.

"The radar gun must have been broken."

The first speeding ticket in a young driver's life can be very traumatic, especially to parents who tend to react badly to the inevitable 9,000 percent increase in insurance premiums. Knowing this, the teen looks to place blame anywhere but on herself.

"I have rights too, you know!"

{ Teenagers get downright indignant when they feel their rights as citizens are being violated. These would include: }

132

the right to watch
TV for seventeen hours in a row

the right to sleep
until three in the afternoon

the right to spend
hundreds of your hard-earned dollars
on essentials like body gel

"Oh ... my ... gawd!"

The typical teenage girl uses this ism (or its hyperactive counterpart: "Omigod, omigod, omigod!") approximately 178 times per day. It can mean anything from "That's the most astounding gossip I've ever heard!" to "Ick! Broccoli!"

"I was only going five miles over the speed limit!"

Your teenage son roars into your driveway at a rate of speed seen only on NASCAR race-tracks. His wheels are a blur and all you can hear is the deafening *thump-thump-thump* of his subwoofer. You accuse him of breaking the sound barrier.

134

He answers with the above ism.

Your ears are ringing too much to argue with him.

"This is a violation of child-labor laws!"

Pity the poor parents whose child is taking a high school civics class. Typically used as an objection to performing the expected household chores like raking the yard and taking out the trash, this ism will have your youngster comparing his plight to that of the young Taiwanese sweatshop worker.

135

Yes, a little knowledge
is a dangerous thing.

"I heard you the first time!"

Just when you're ready to schedule an appointment for a full audiological screening because your teenage child has not responded to thirty-seven consecutive requests to take out the trash, and you're convinced he has become deaf in both ears from too many hip-hop concerts, you will hear this retort—loud and clear.

136

"Of course his parents are going to be home."

When hearing this kind of reassurance from your teen, it's often a good idea to ask him to define "home." Some teens' definition of home means the Sandals resort in Bali.

137

"Can I borrow the car keys?"

This ism strikes fear into the hearts of parents no matter how complete their insurance coverage. Somehow, kids have come to the conclusion that asking to "borrow the keys" is a little less intimidating than saying, "Dad, can I back your car out of the driveway at record speed, run the reds over to Jason's house, and play chicken on County Road 4 until the tires blow?"

"Whatever."

{ **Translation:** I can't think of a killer comeback right now, so I'm playing the aloof card—again. }

"I dunno."

As smart as teens want us to believe they are, they often seem to lack the most basic information. The average teen utters this ism 14.8 times per day. Examples:

140

Q: What did you do in school today?
A: *I dunno.*

Q: How's your grade in chemistry?
A: *I dunno.*

Q: Who are you going to ask to prom?
A: *I dunno.*

Q: Is there anything you *do* know?
A: *Huh?*

"We're just friends."

The last thing a teenager wants in the world is for his parents to know he is in a romantic relationship. Because that opens the barn door for a barrage of questions: "Who is she?" "What do her parents do?" Not to mention the inevitable "talk" between father and son that is supposed to prevent pregnancy, social diseases, and shotgun weddings.

This is why kids will insist "we're just friends" until just moments before they walk down the aisle at their wedding.

"I'm not a kid anymore, you know."

This declarative statement is typically used when a dad is staring—gape-mouthed and dumbfounded—at his teenage daughter modeling her new bathing suit, which leaves nothing to the imagination but the brand of tanning lotion she's wearing.

If he can manage to spit out the words, "Where do you think you're going in that?" chances are he'll get the above reply.

142

"None of your business."

A parent's job is to pry as much information as possible out of her teen. A teen's job is to withhold as much information as he can. If this were not the case, parents and teens would have nothing to do in life.

"*!%$#!!"

In a world where the Osbournes and potty mouths of *South Park* have *bleep*ed their way to fame and fortune, your kid's first cuss word was bound to happen. And, unless you yourself possess the vocabulary of a landlocked sailor, the first *f*-bomb or *s*-word can come as quite a shock. But that's the point, isn't it? To shock? Of course, it is. And that's precisely why you should nip such offensive language in the bud.

At the first utterance of a four-letter word, experts recommend isolating the child in a room with no other stimuli but *The Brady Bunch* and *Leave It to Beaver* reruns for six to eight weeks.

Caution: This treatment may backfire, leaving a child's vocabulary drastically reduced to equally annoying phrases like: "That's groovy, in a far-out happening way" and "What a lovely dress, Mrs. Cleaver!"

"I like my hair this way!"

{ There are so few things teens have power over. One of them is their hair. A word of advice: Let 'em have this one. It will always grow back. }

"But everybody's wearing them to school!"

A common retort to a parent's mandate, "You're not going to school looking like that," this teenism is an attempt to reassure said parent that belly-button rings, fishnet stockings, or sheer tube tops are de rigueur at her educational institution.

147

"I don't have any clothes."

A teenage girl can have mountains of jeans, sweaters, T-shirts, panties, and bras covering every inch of her bedroom floor and, still, she'll have no problem voicing the above complaint. This ism has been known to cause temporary insanity in mothers whose check-book registers show hundreds of dollars spent at the Gap.

148

"We were just hanging out."

Formerly known as loitering, "hanging out" is the act of sitting or standing around in a dark environment at least five hundred yards from the nearest adult and doing absolutely nothing.

"We were just talking."

You've come home late to find your daughter and her date in a car parked in front of your house. The windows are fogged, and your three attempts to knock on the window are met with nothing but silence. When she finally surfaces, your little girl looks like Tammy Faye Bakker with tousled hair, smeared mascara, and disheveled clothing. "What were you doing in there?" you ask in shock. This ism will be her answer. And unless you're a total dip wad, you'll know they were doing anything *but* talking.

"It was just a little toilet paper…"

The phone rings at one A.M. It's police Sergeant O'Brien informing you that Principal Henry's eight mature pin oak trees are now festively draped in what appears to be fifteen cases of Charmin. Principal Henry is considering pressing charges, and your son, who was caught redhanded in mid–hook shot, can only come up with the above excuse.

It is then that you realize it was not your imagination when the toilet paper seemed to disappear into thin air all those weeks prior, and that you owe your husband a big apology.

"I just had a few ships."

{ Your teen has just returned from a night out with his friends. The distinctive aroma of cheap beer is on his breath, and he's wearing that dopey grin you've seen only once, just before he went under for his tonsillectomy. }

152

The few "ships" he claimed
to have had must've been
bigger than the **QE2**.

"Other people were drinking, but not me!"

Sometimes you have to wonder how your child can keep the glow of his halo from blinding the other kids around him.

"I learned my lesson. Really."

{ A teen's attempt at remorse can tug at your heartstrings—*for about ten seconds*! }

"Just ... forget it!"

{ This common bail-out is a sure sign your child senses he is losing the argument. Try not to jump up and down until he has completely exited the room. }

"I'll be home by midnight."

{ Your definition of midnight: 12:00 A.M. sharp

Their definition of midnight: 12:00 to 3:00 A.M., not including drive time. }

"Don't wait up."

Here's something fun to try:

The first time your teen says "Don't wait up!" answer "Okay, I was sleepy anyway!" Then immediately consume enough coffee, cola, or No-Doz tablets to stay up till next Wednesday. Then, when she comes in at three in the morning, simply tell her you couldn't sleep, and let the interrogation begin!

157

"I would never wear anything of yours!"

{ Isn't it interesting how your daughter claims she would rather *die* than wear anything of yours when, on any given day, you can find shoes, jeans, lipstick, sweatpants, mascara, and your favorite sweater on the floor in the back of her closet? }

158

"I know I didn't go to school today. I feel better now. Why can't I go out?"

It's a miraculous thing to see a child who was so ill that he could hardly sit up, much less take a chemistry exam, rally to make a football game that very same night.

159

It's a modern medical miracle, that's what it is.

"Could I borrow ten dollars?"

Do you ever wonder why a child asks to "borrow" money, when he hasn't the slightest intention of paying it back? The reason is, "borrowing" sounds much better than "Could I spend ten dollars of your hard-earned money in the most foolish ways you can imagine?"

160

That's why.

"Do you have any money?"

{ When kids use this approach, rest assured, they're not interested in your current state of economic security. They are trying to determine the maximum amount available for "borrowing." }

"This is so lame, stupid, or pathetic."

{ The difference between *lame, stupid,* and *pathetic* is extremely subtle. Perhaps these examples will help you out: }

Going to a movie with your family is lame.

Going to a G-rated movie is stupid.

Going to a G-rated movie with your family on a Saturday night when everybody else is sneaking into *Scary Movie 3* is pathetic.

"I'm going to the library."

Try not to laugh too hard the first time your teen pulls this one on you. It was funny enough back in the days when some kids actually *went* to the library, but in the age of web surfing, CD-ROMs, and online term papers, this one should raise all kinds of red flags.

163

"I'll be at the mall."

Unlike the library, when your teen says she'll be at the mall, you can believe her. Just be sure to conduct a full body search for your credit cards before she leaves the house.

"I'm going to Amy's to study."

{ Okay, maybe it's *possible* he's really going to Amy's, and maybe studying is somewhere on the agenda. }

But I doubt it.

And so should you.

"Did you have sex with Dad before you got married?"

There are two questions dreaded by every parent who grew up after 1969. One is the above teenism. The immediate response is to deny, of course, that you and your spouse were *ever* sexually intimate, making the birth of your child the second documented immaculate conception in the history of man.

166

Kids won't question this response, since no kid wants to entertain the idea of their parents "in that way."

"Have you ever smoked pot?"

This is the second. Parents who came of age during the 1960s or 1970s will quake in their desert boots at this shocking yet inevitable question. The jury's still out on the best way to answer it. Some advocate the honest approach while others think it's best to take such information to the grave, along with their macramé vests and black-light posters.

"You did it and you turned out okay."

If there is an argument against total honesty between parent and child, it is the above observation. In the spirit of complete candor, you can confess to smoking, drinking, inhaling, driving fast, sleeping around ... all with some lame excuse about it being the 1960s or '70s ("times were different ... we didn't know what we know today"), and your child will turn it around and use it to bolster his case for doing the same dumb stuff.

168

"You just don't understand."

Alas. Pity the misunderstood teenager who, try as she might, can never convey the real tragedy of her circumstance.

The most effective response to this one is "I understand more than you think!"

That'll really get her worried.

169

"That's a stupid rule!"

{ Most kids would agree that there is no such thing as a "smart" rule. And here, in no particular order, are the Top Ten stupidest rules in a teen's eyes. }

1. Feet off the table.

2. If you stay home from school, you can't go out that night.

3. Elbows off the table.

4. No TV until your homework is done.

5. Always wear a bra to school.

6. Knees off the table.

7. Limit phone calls to ten minutes
on school nights.

8. No overnight guests of the opposite sex.

9. No phone calls after ten o'clock.

10. Hands on the wheel at 10 and 2.

"My kids will never be grounded for a whole weekend."

When a kid makes this indignant declaration, be sure to document it on paper and have her sign and date it at the bottom. Then, save it for her wedding day and give it to her with your grandmother's locket.

172

"You are so overprotective."

Overprotective, as opposed to simply protective, usually means a reluctance to send your underage child in a car with other underage children to a Mexican border town for spring break with no chaperones.

"I'm spending the night at Jennifer's."

Danger! Danger! Warning! Warning!

When you hear this ism casually tossed out as your teen is leaving the house, especially on prom or graduation night, do *not* pass go, do *not* hesitate. Get on the phone and call Jennifer's parents to confirm they exist and that they're expecting company.

"Jennifer's" could be your child's code word for the Holiday Inn.

"Sure, she/he's a good driver."

Your definition of good driver: Wears seatbelts at all times. Earned straight As in driver's ed. Holds a 4.0 GPA with aspirations of attending Harvard Med. No moving violations. Hands at 10 and 2. Drives five miles under the speed limit at all times. Always uses turn signal. No stereo in car.

Your teen's definition of good driver: Can take a turn at 90 mph without flipping over.

"I got it! It's for me!"

{ Like a shotgun signaling the start of a race, a ringing phone can turn a teenage girl into an Olympic hurdler, flying over furniture and lunging for the receiver at the finish line. }

"I'm expecting a very important call!"

Your definition of a very important call: A communiqué from the doctor, pharmacist, or tax attorney.

Your teen's definition of a very important call: A critical update on the very important developments of an after-school conversation between two very important players in the junior high school scene.

"It's not just a crush, it's *love!*"

Never underestimate the emotional intensity of adolescent attraction. They are just as valid and real as mature relationships. There's nothing more maddening to an eleven-year-old than to have her relationship with Leo DiCaprio reduced to a mere crush. Because what else *but* love would cause a young girl to spend weeks on end pasting Leo photos on top of expensive wallpaper and kissing each one of them before she leaves her room for school every morning?

"Have you been in my room?"

Teens have some kind of built-in radar, an uncanny knack that tells them when an item of clothing has been moved, even a couple inches, from the middle of a pile of clothing four feet high and six feet wide. And don't even think about going through their drawers! Kids can sense a drawer rifling from miles off.

179

"Keep out of my stuff!"

A teenager's stuff is of the utmost importance to him—more important than his friends, family, or pets. To mess with his stuff is to mess with his very soul.

180

"I don't tell *you* what to wear!"

Yes, and thank goodness for that. Otherwise there'd be legions of pierced and tattooed parents at the PTA oozing out of low-rider jeans and cropped tops.

181

"This sucks."

{ **Translation:** This is definitely not acceptable to me. And I feel very strongly about this. }